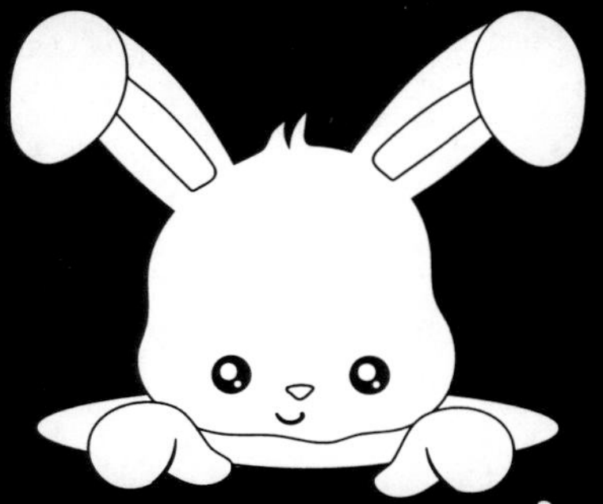

Baby Name

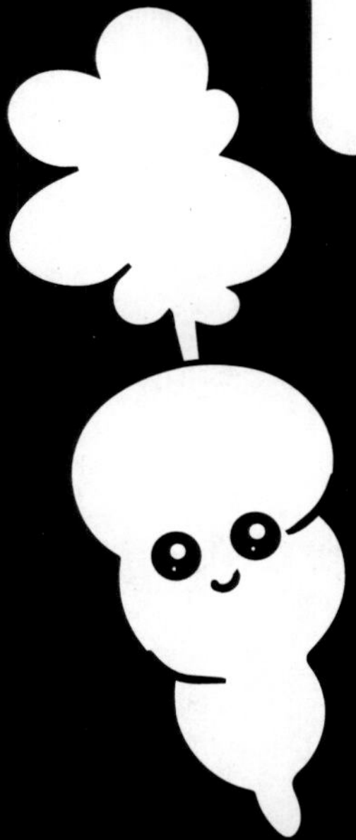

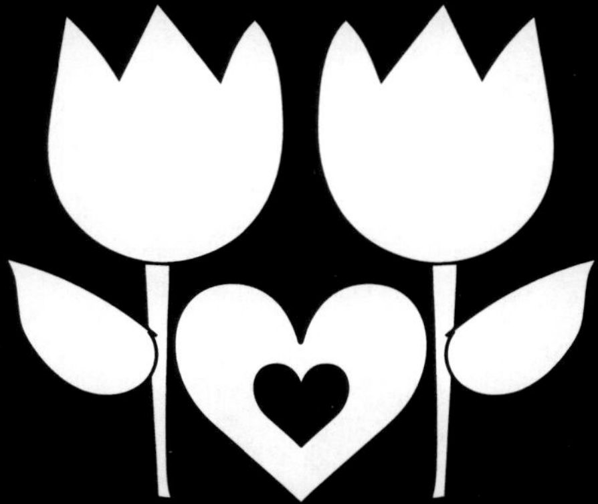

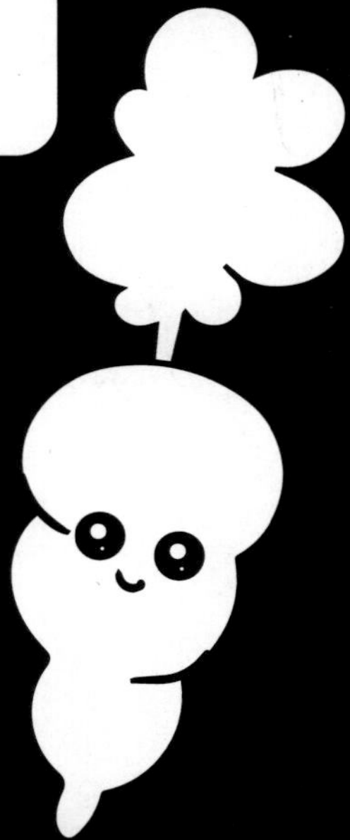

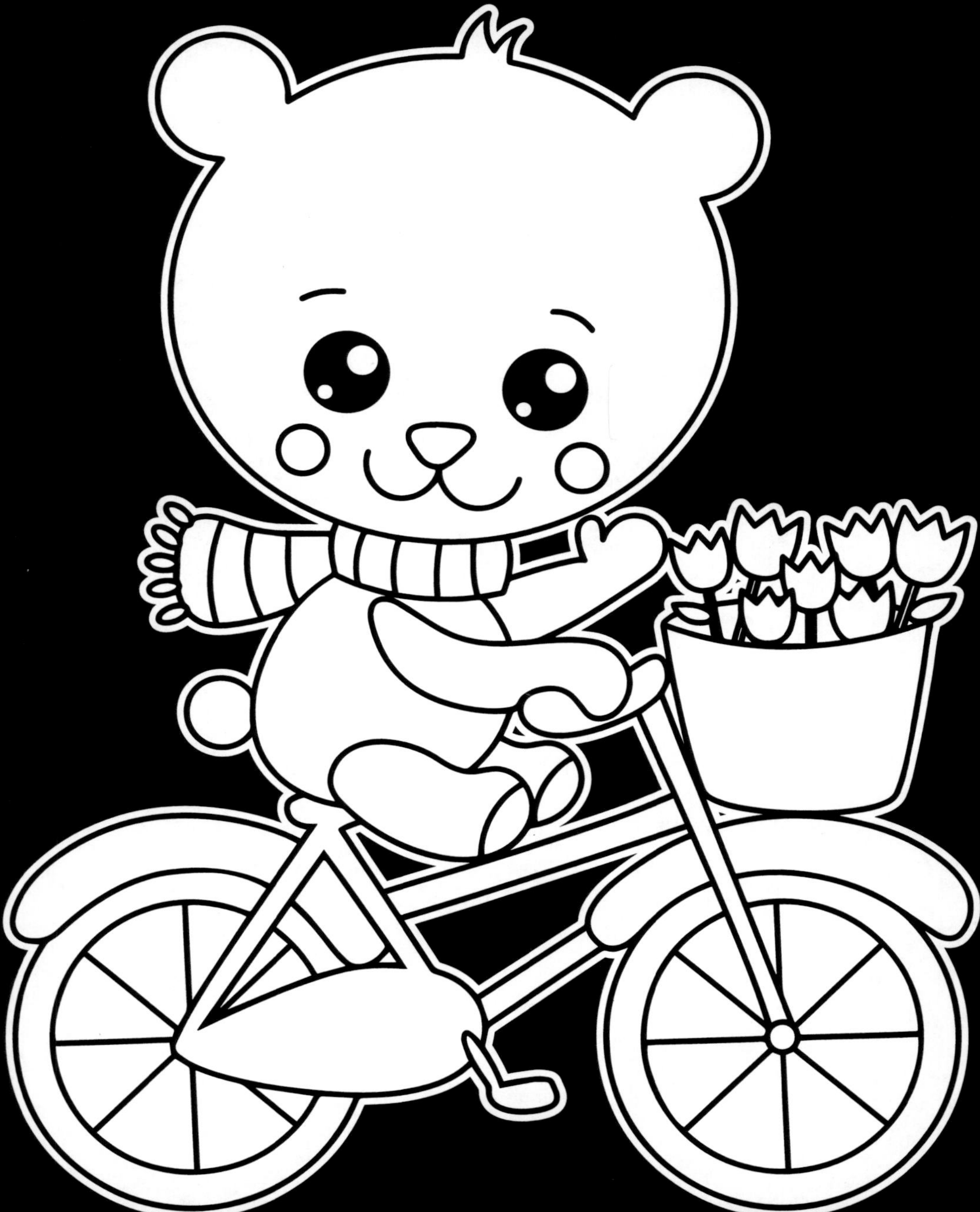

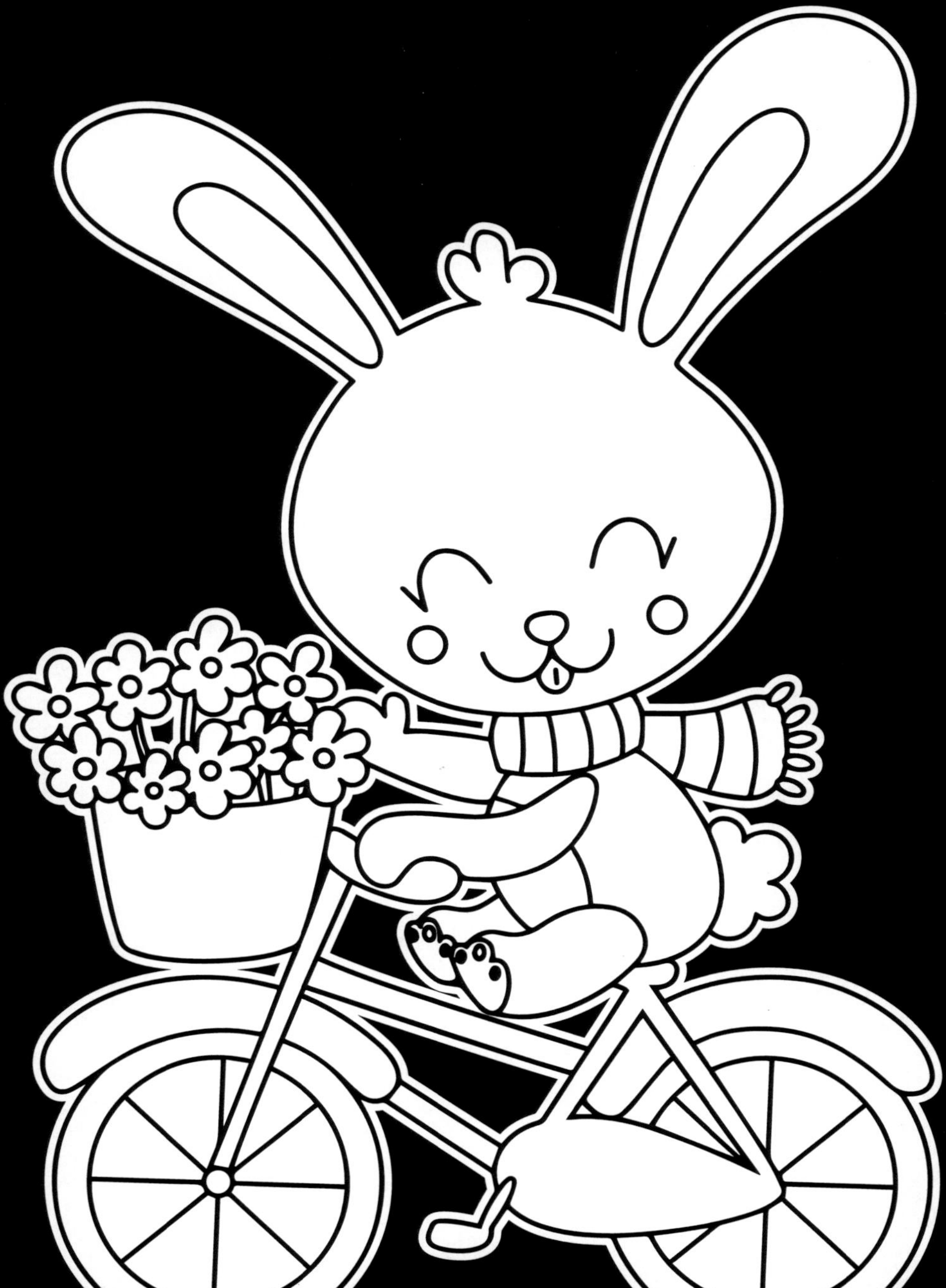

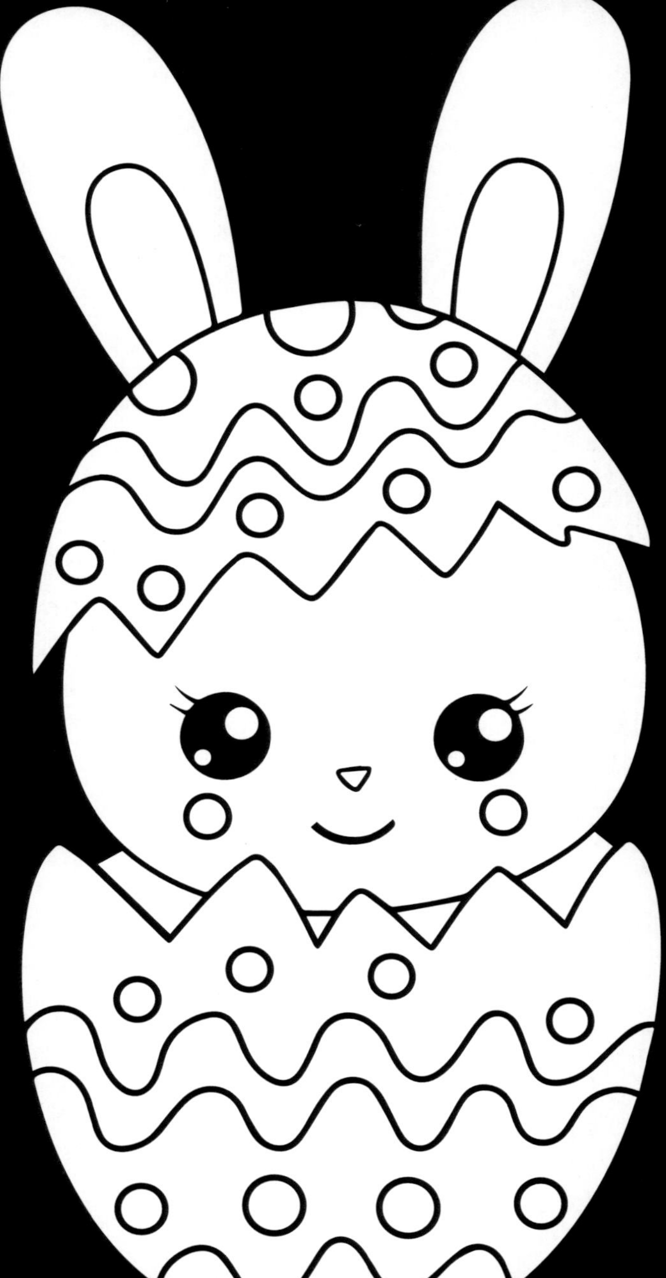

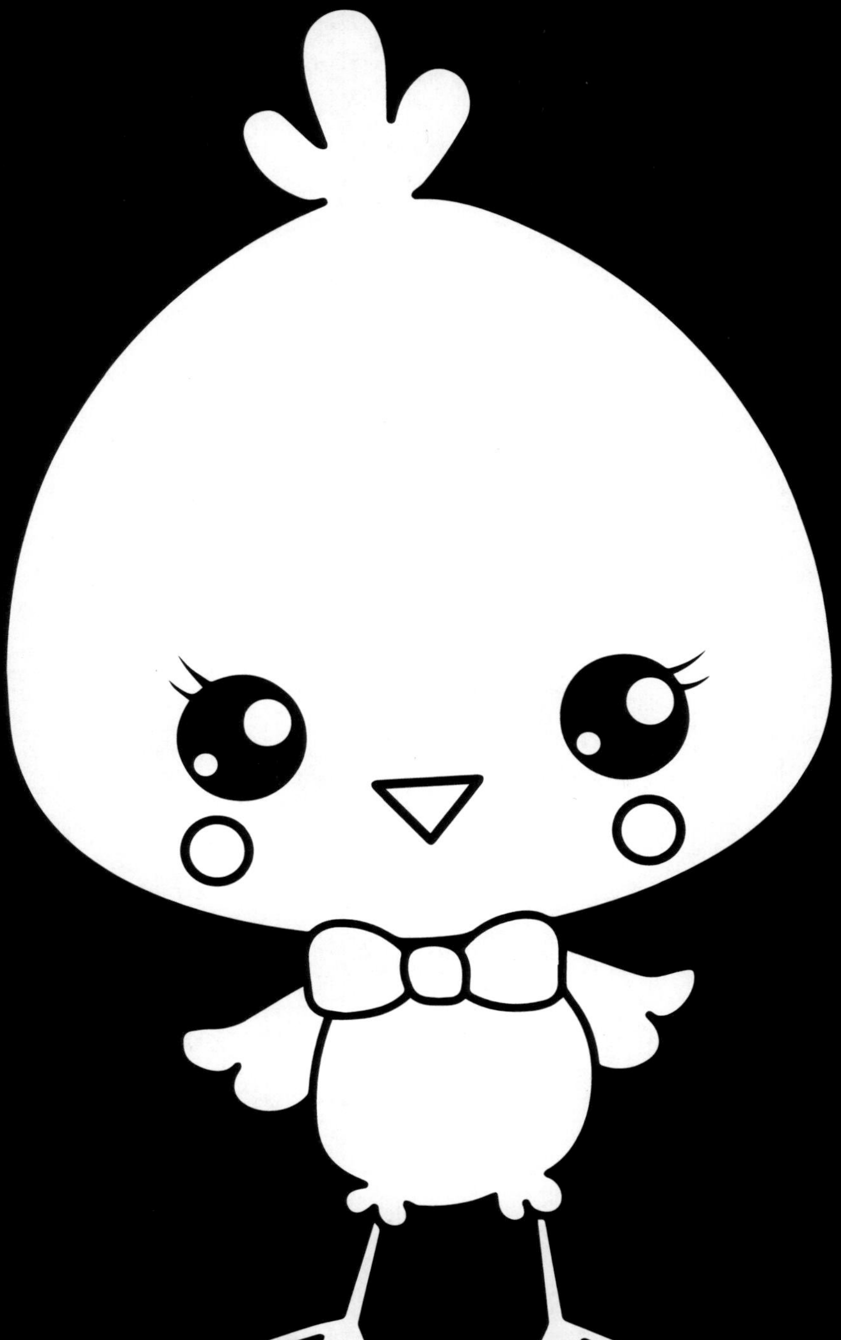

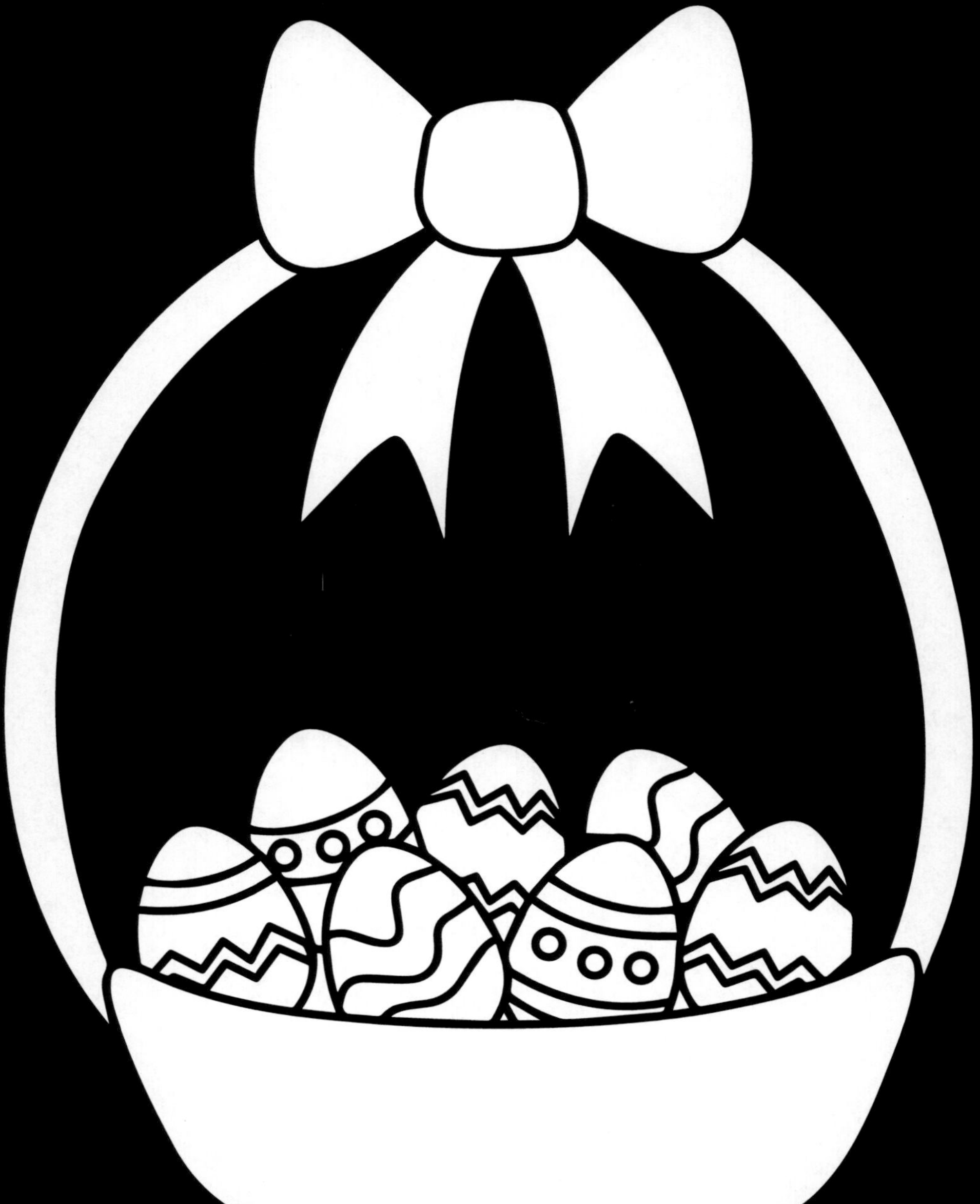

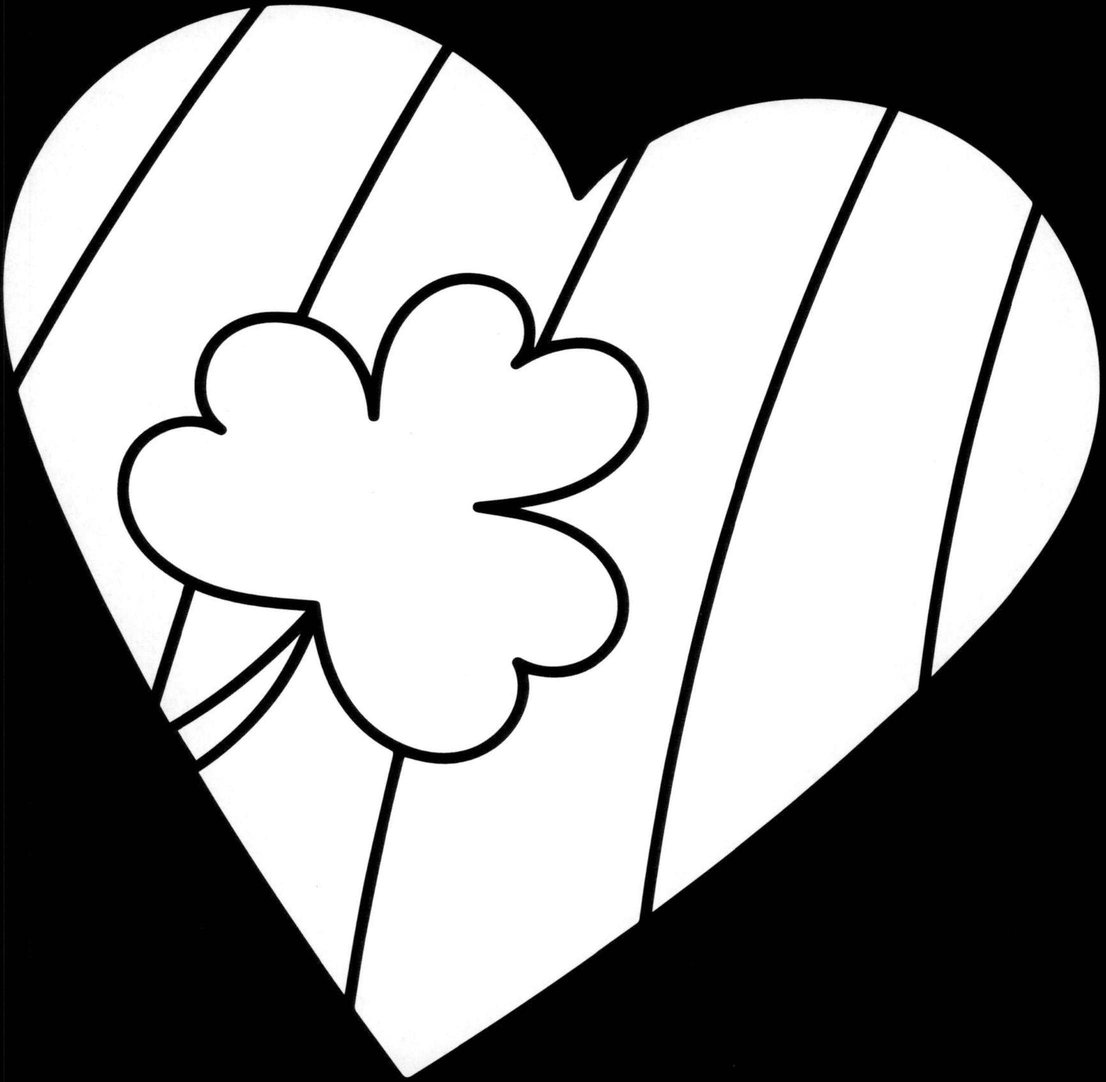

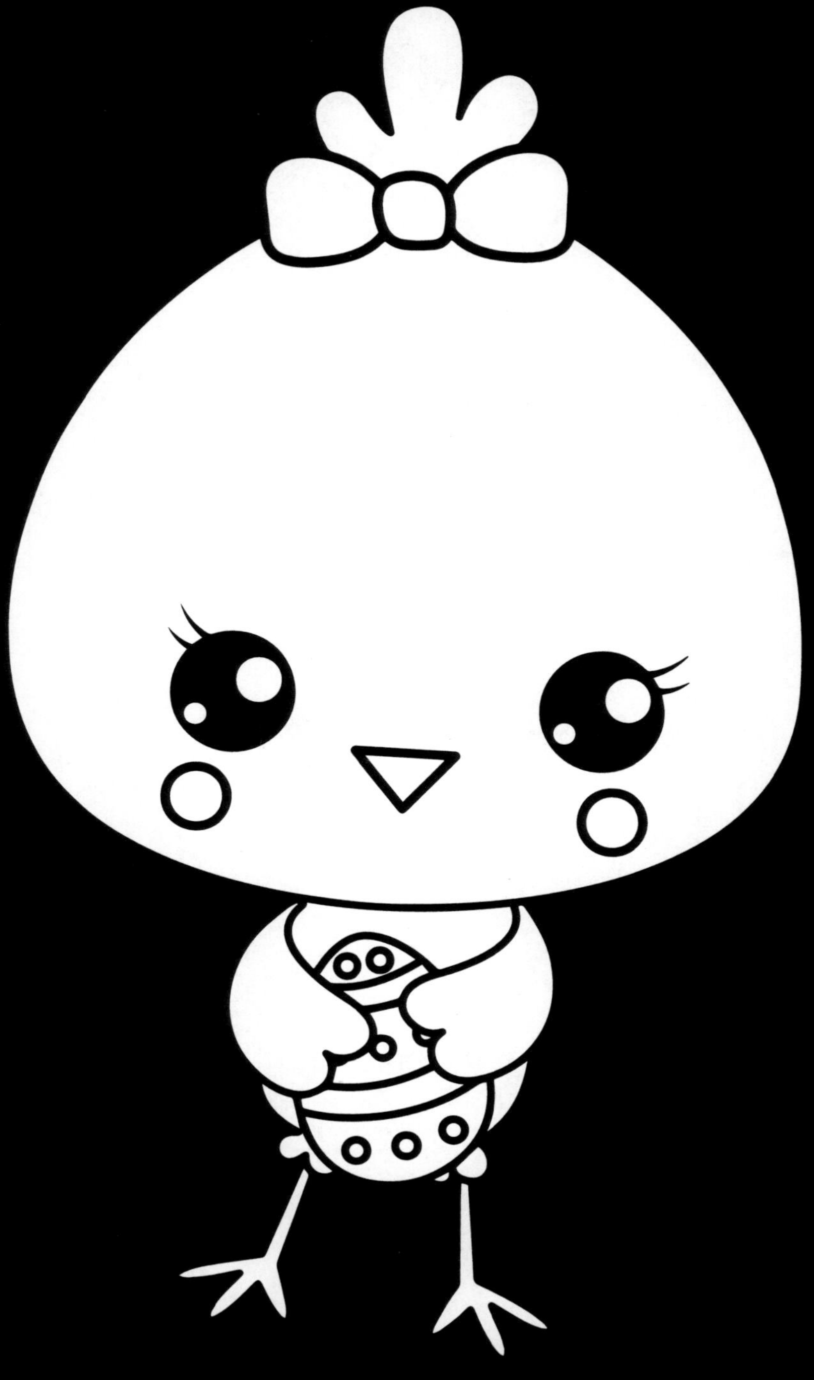

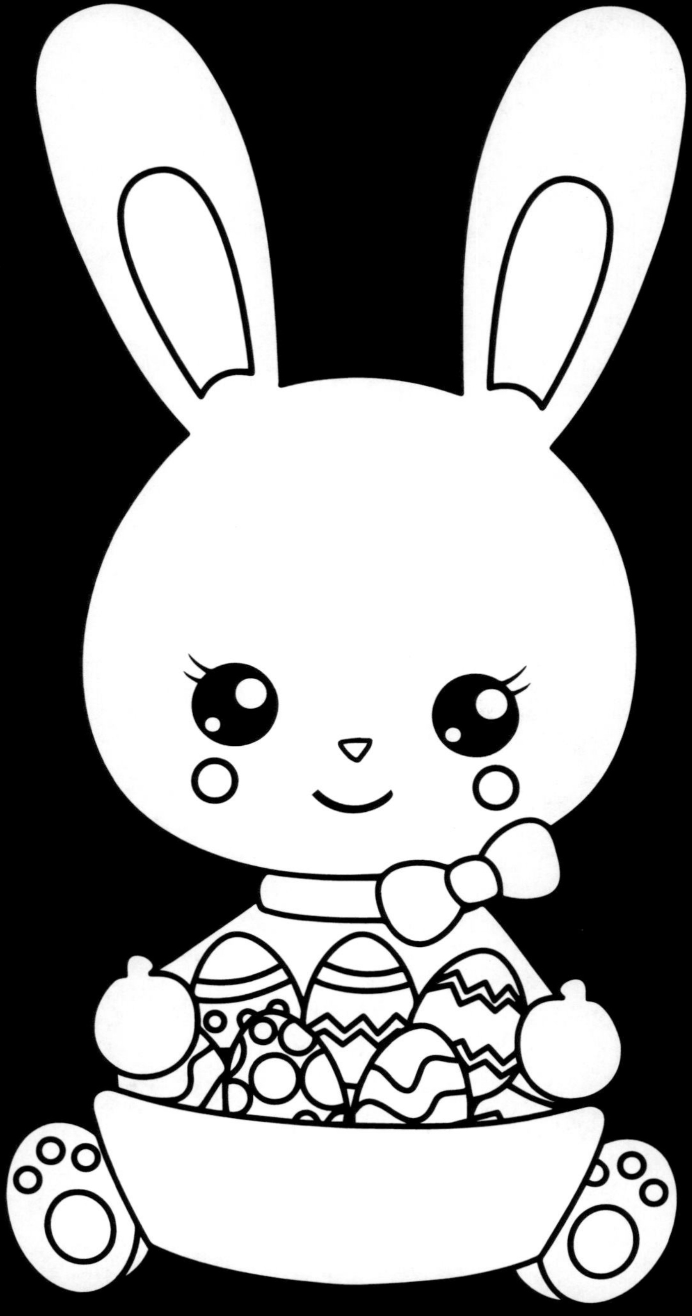

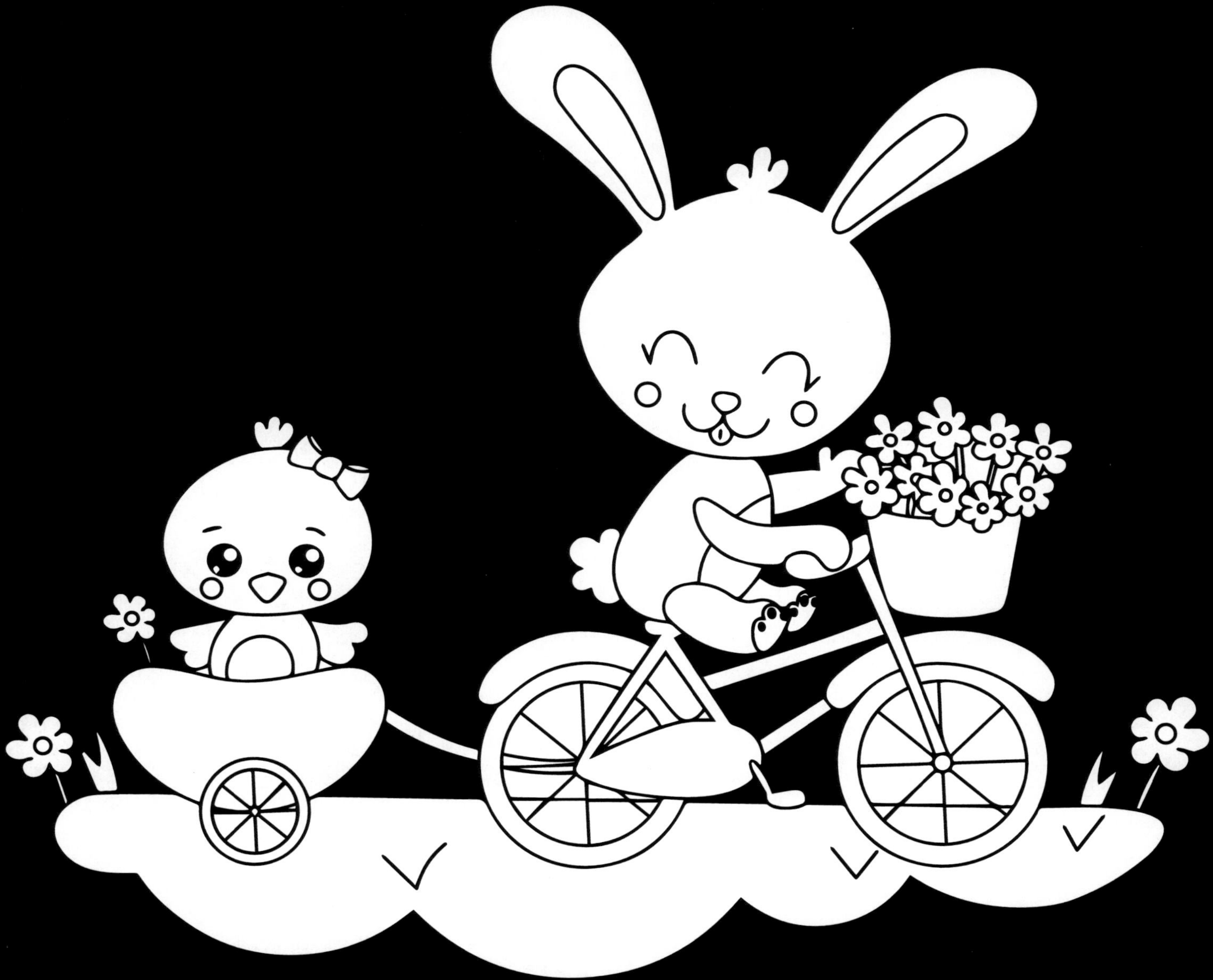

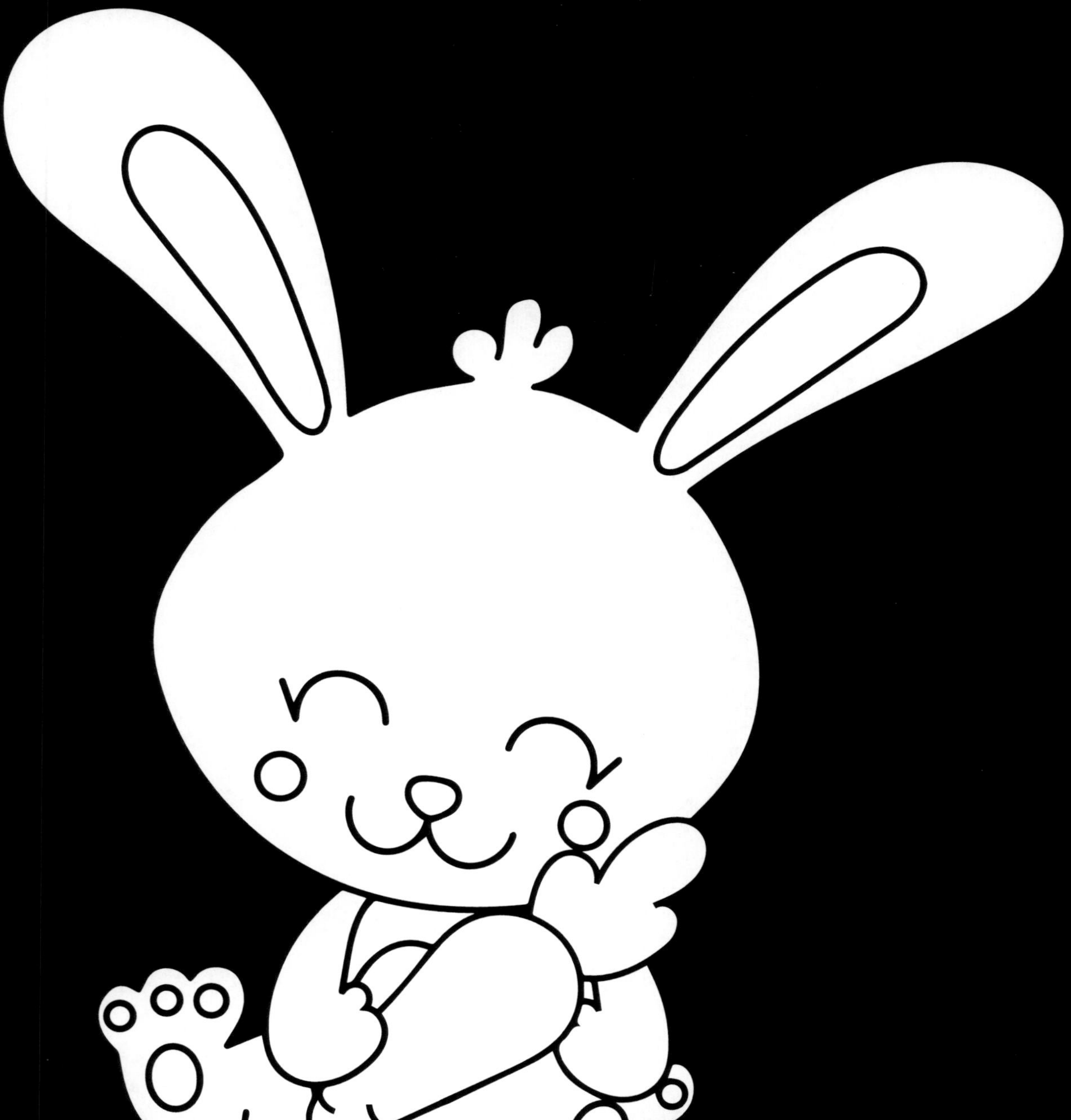

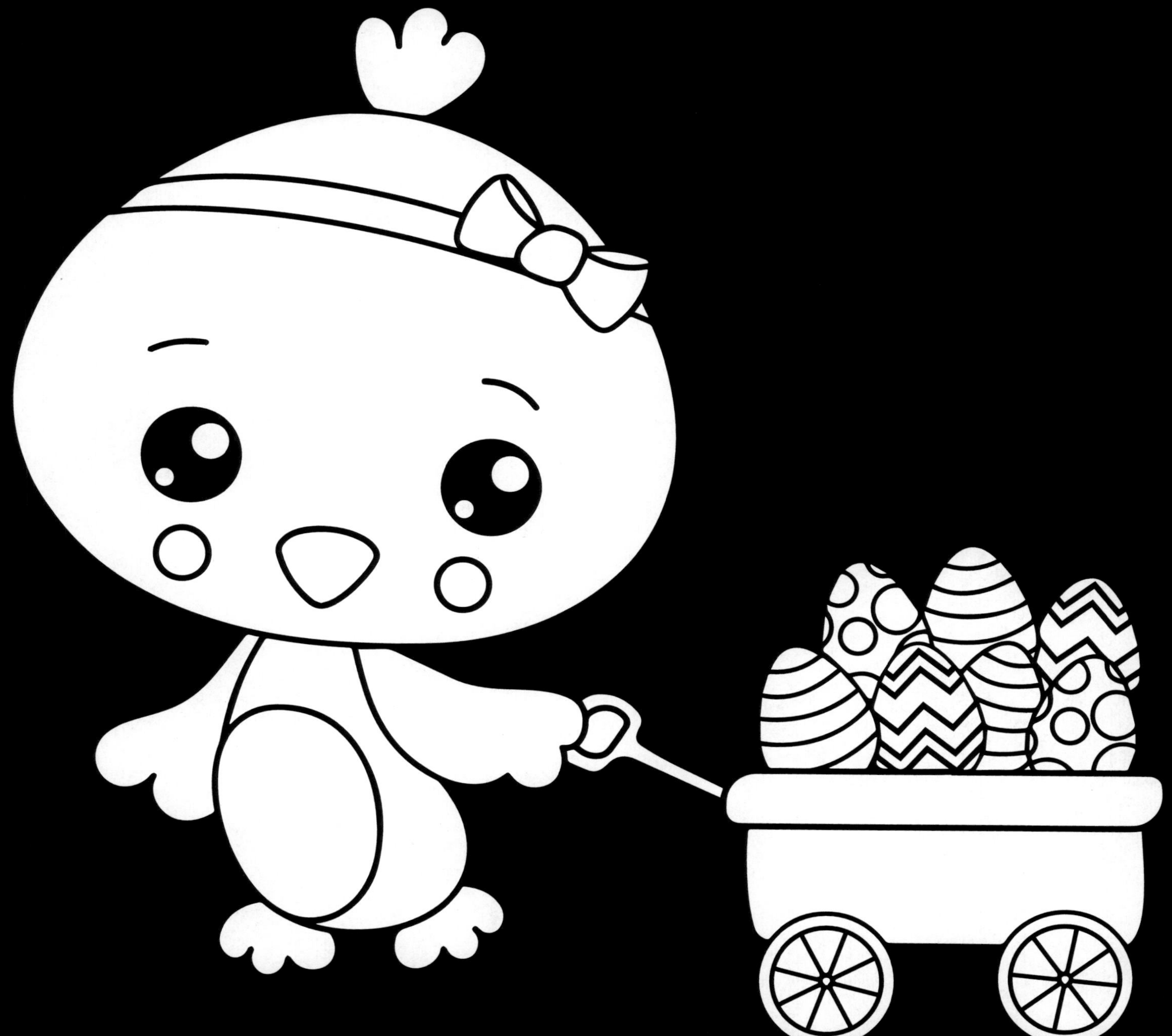

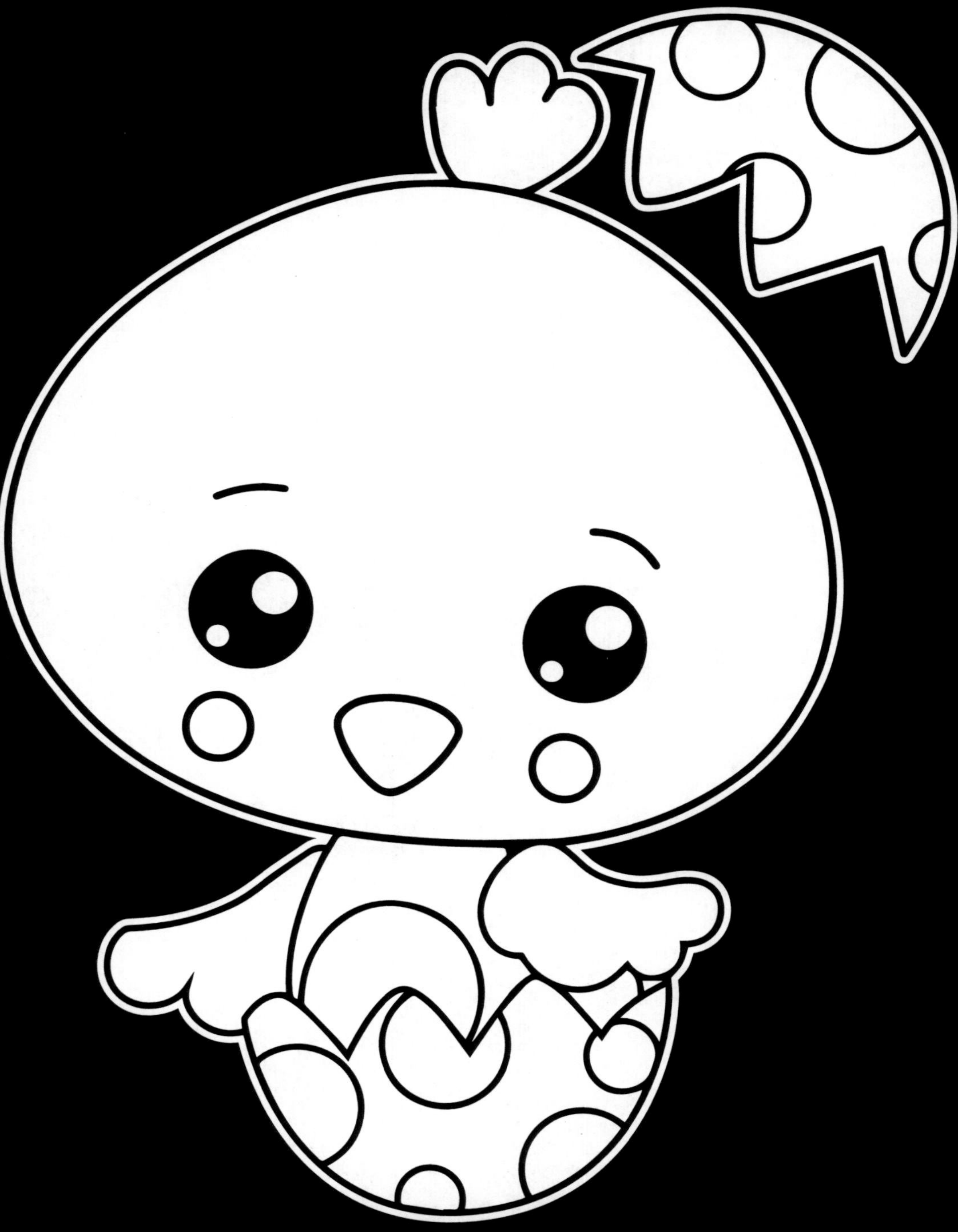

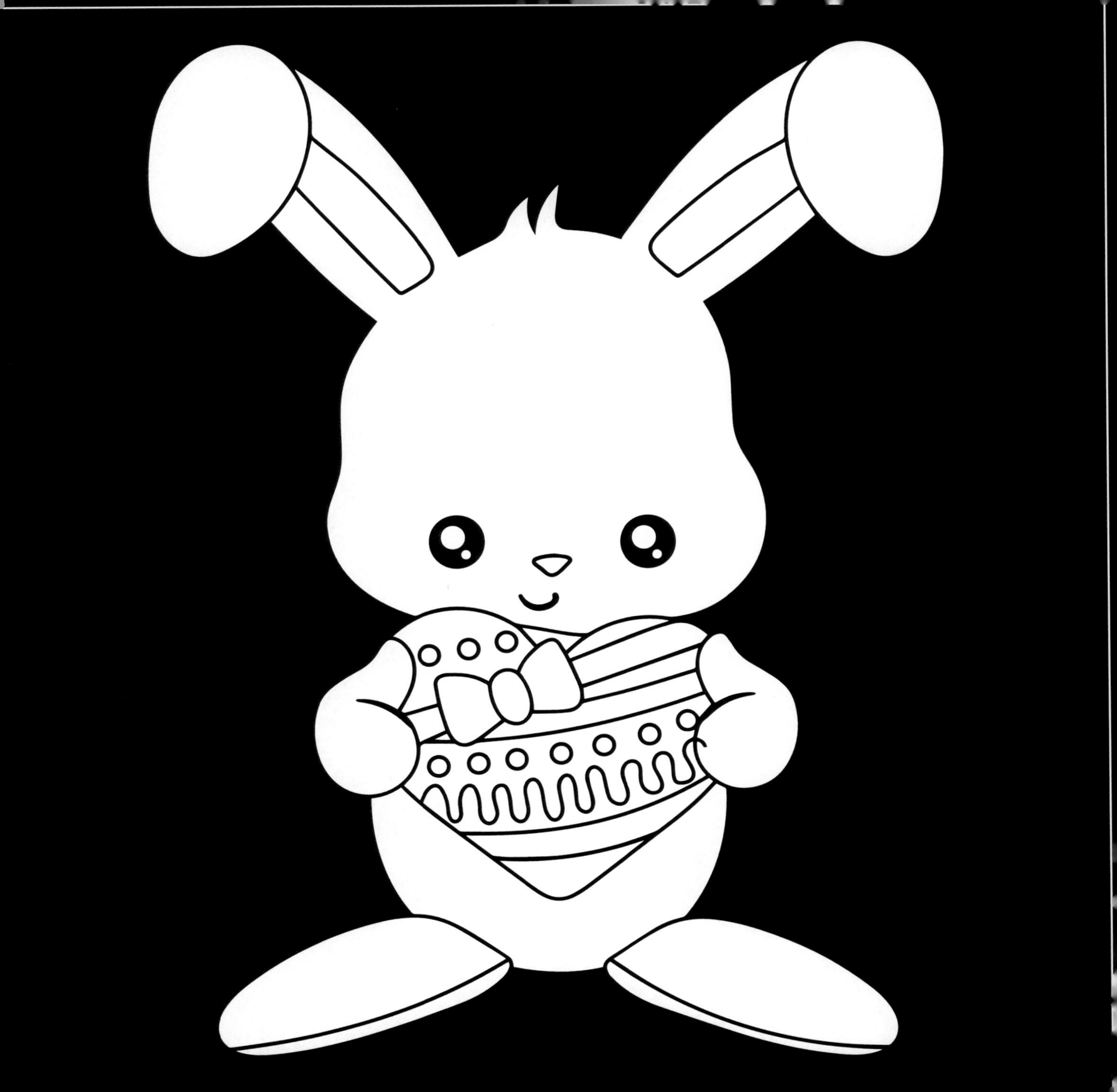

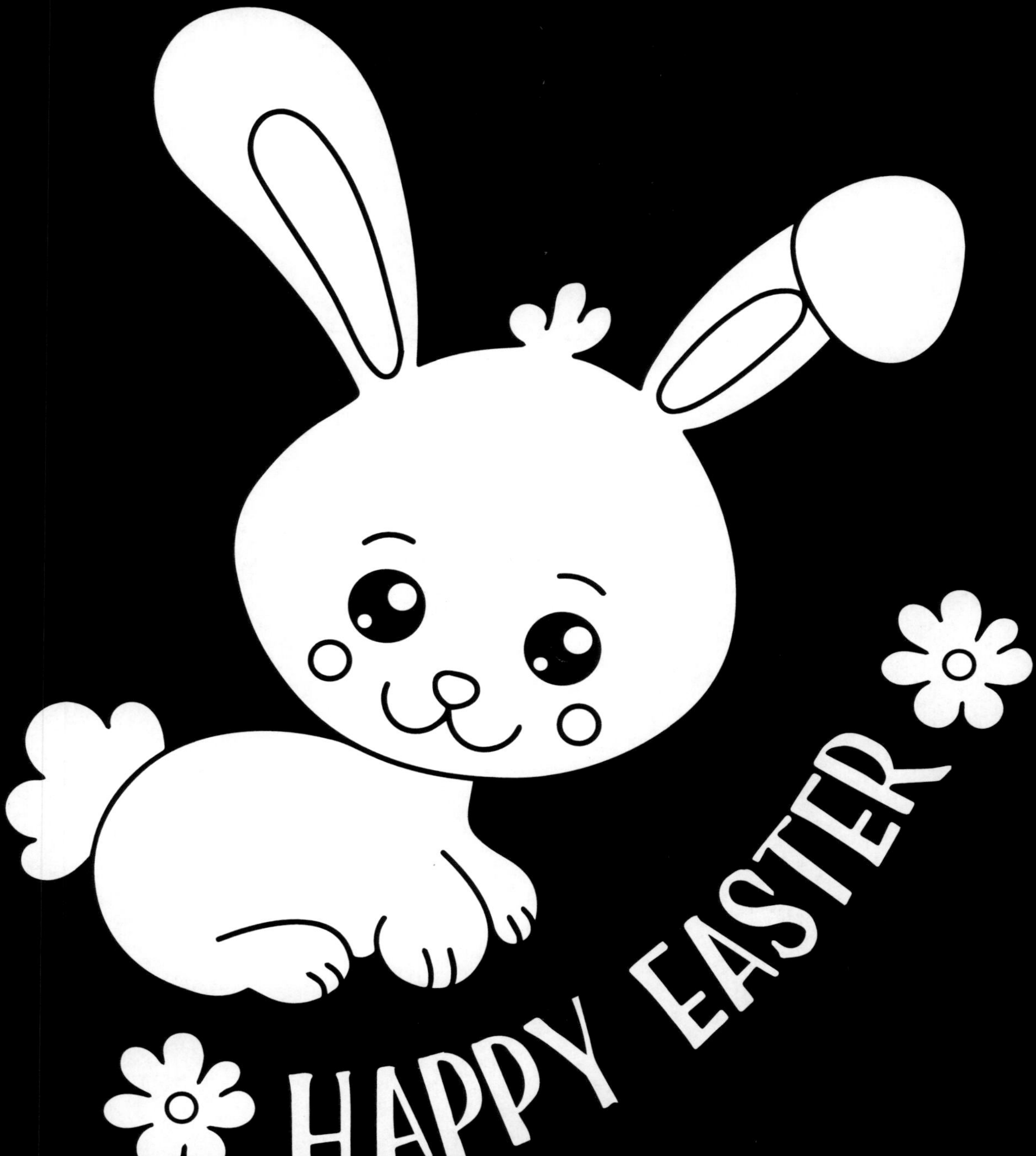
HAPPY EASTER

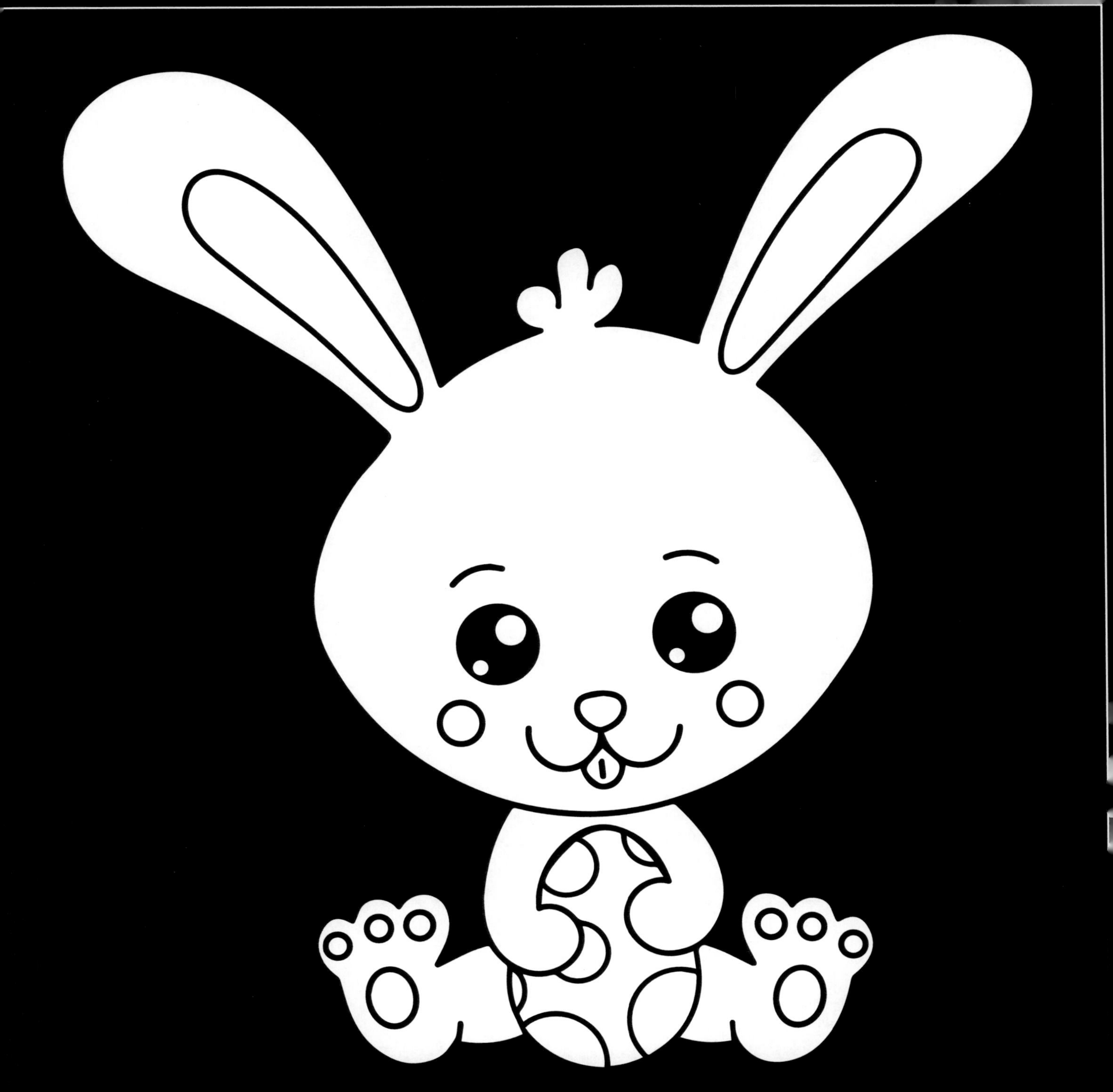

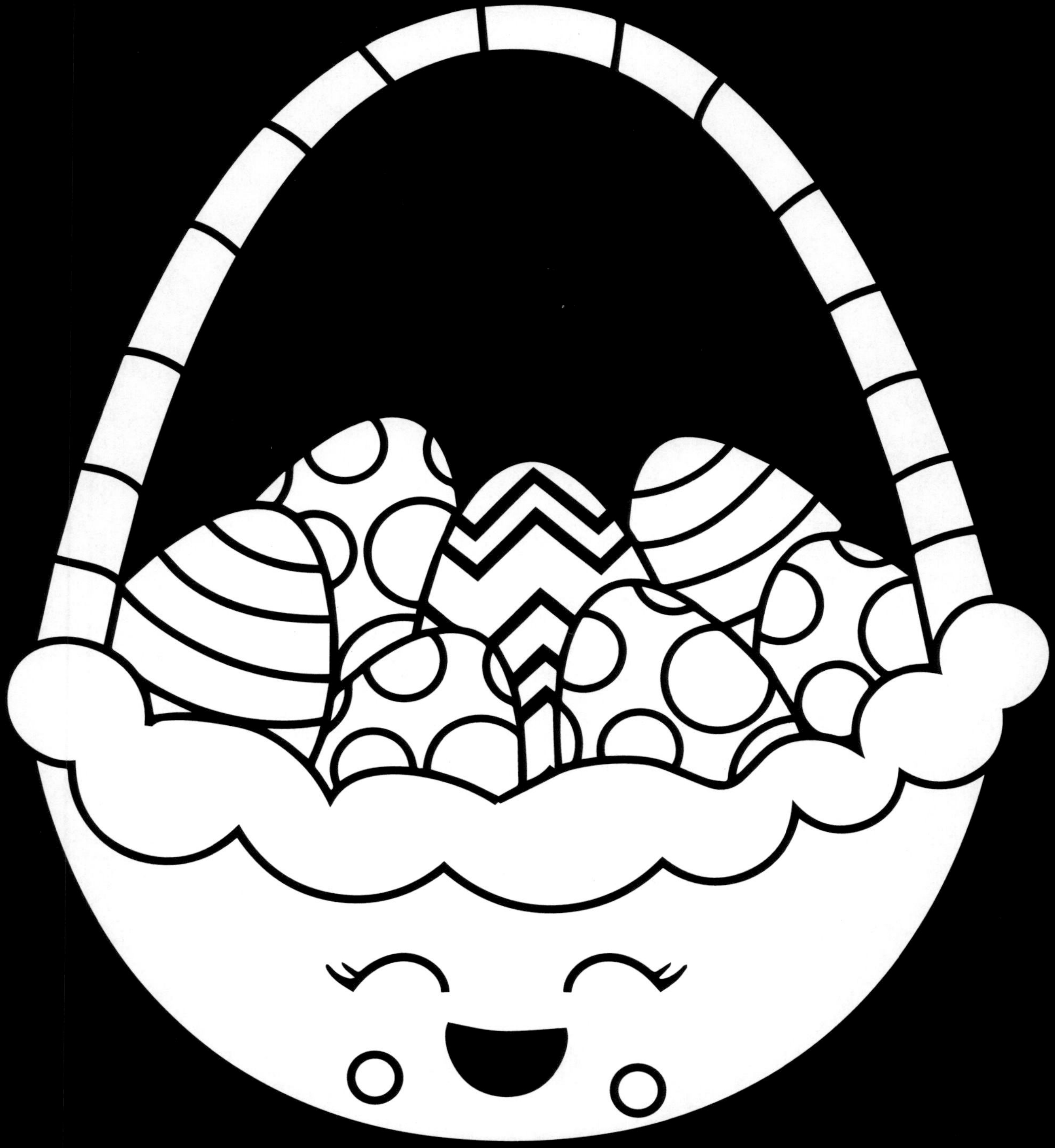

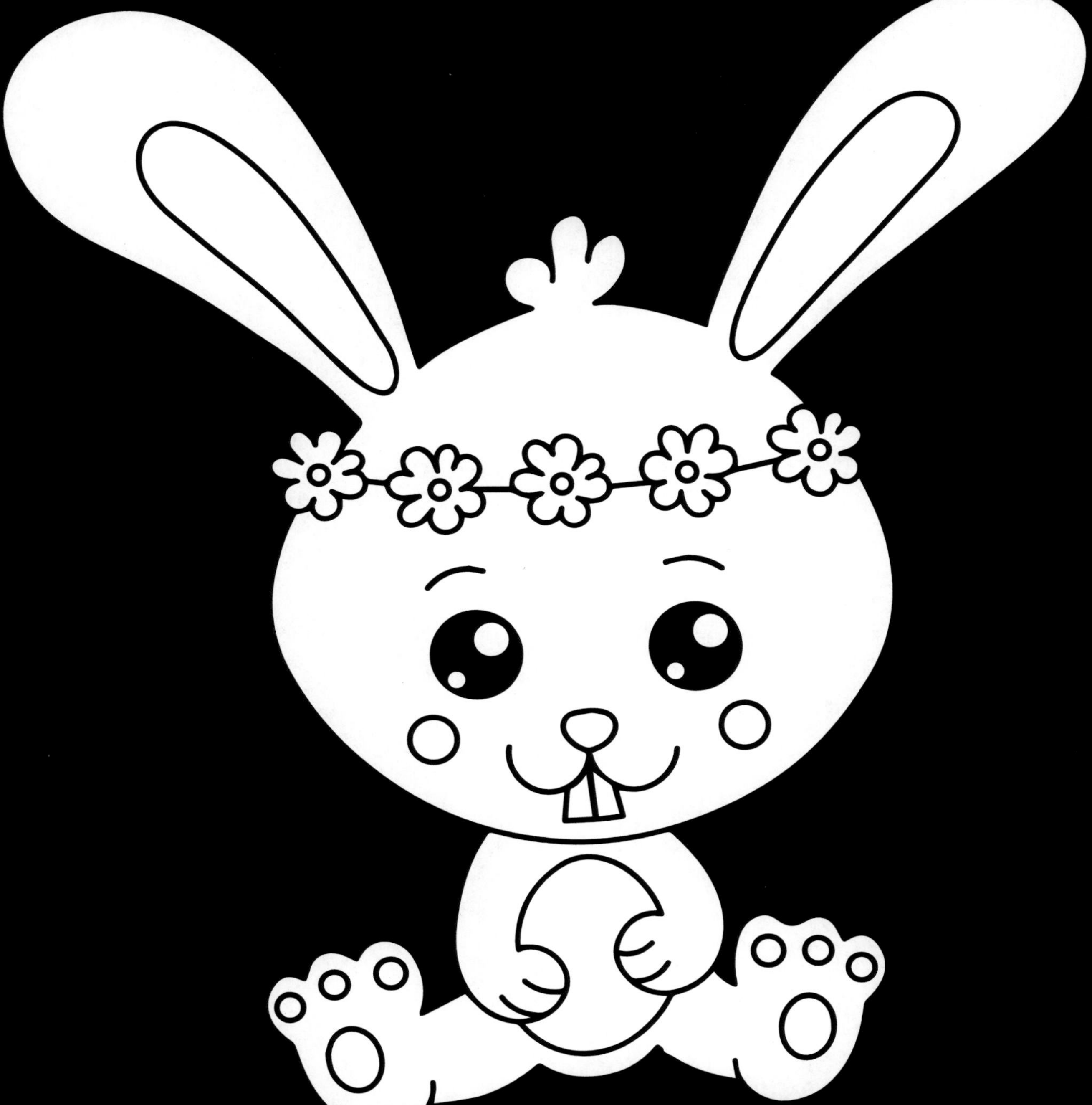

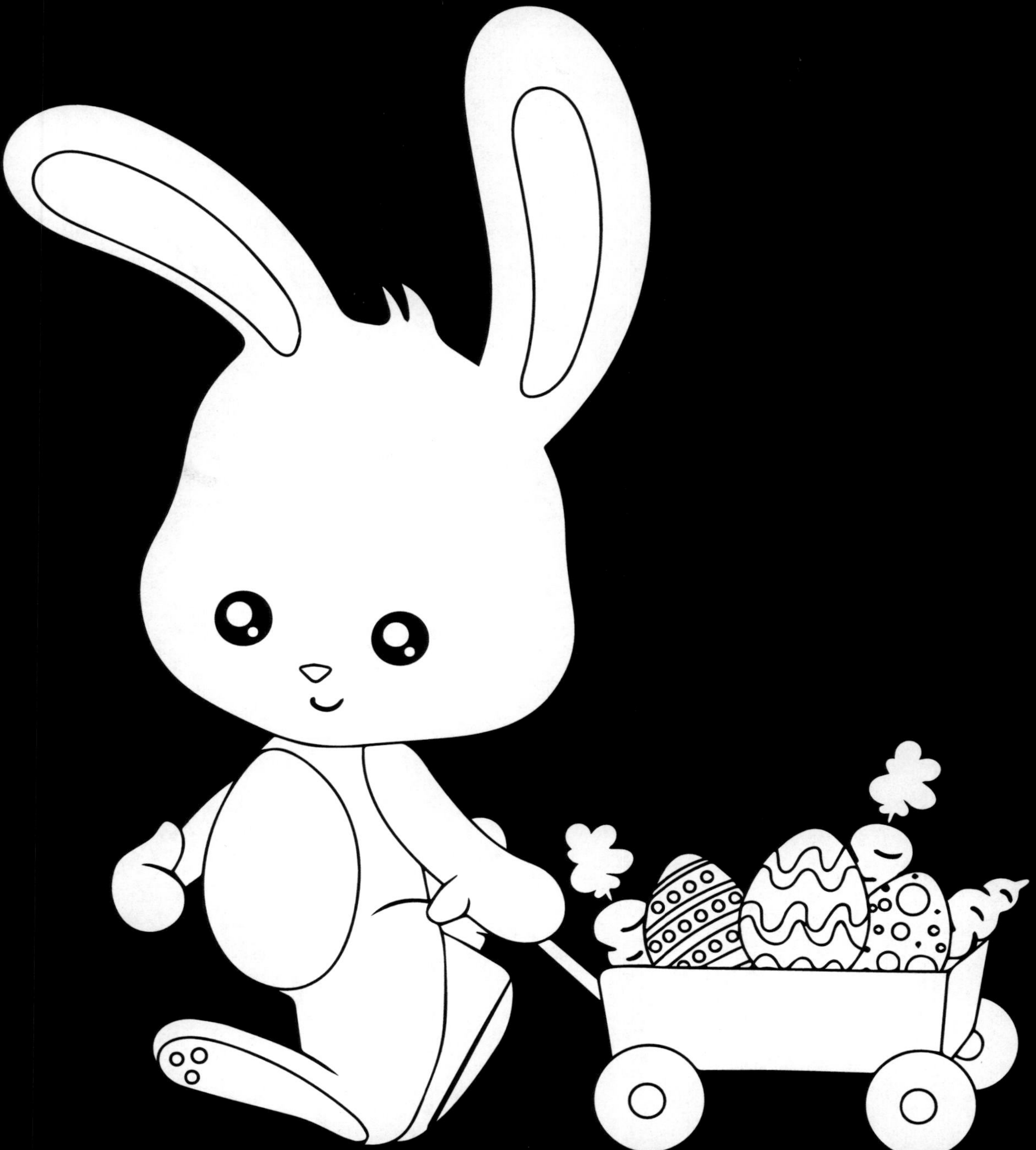

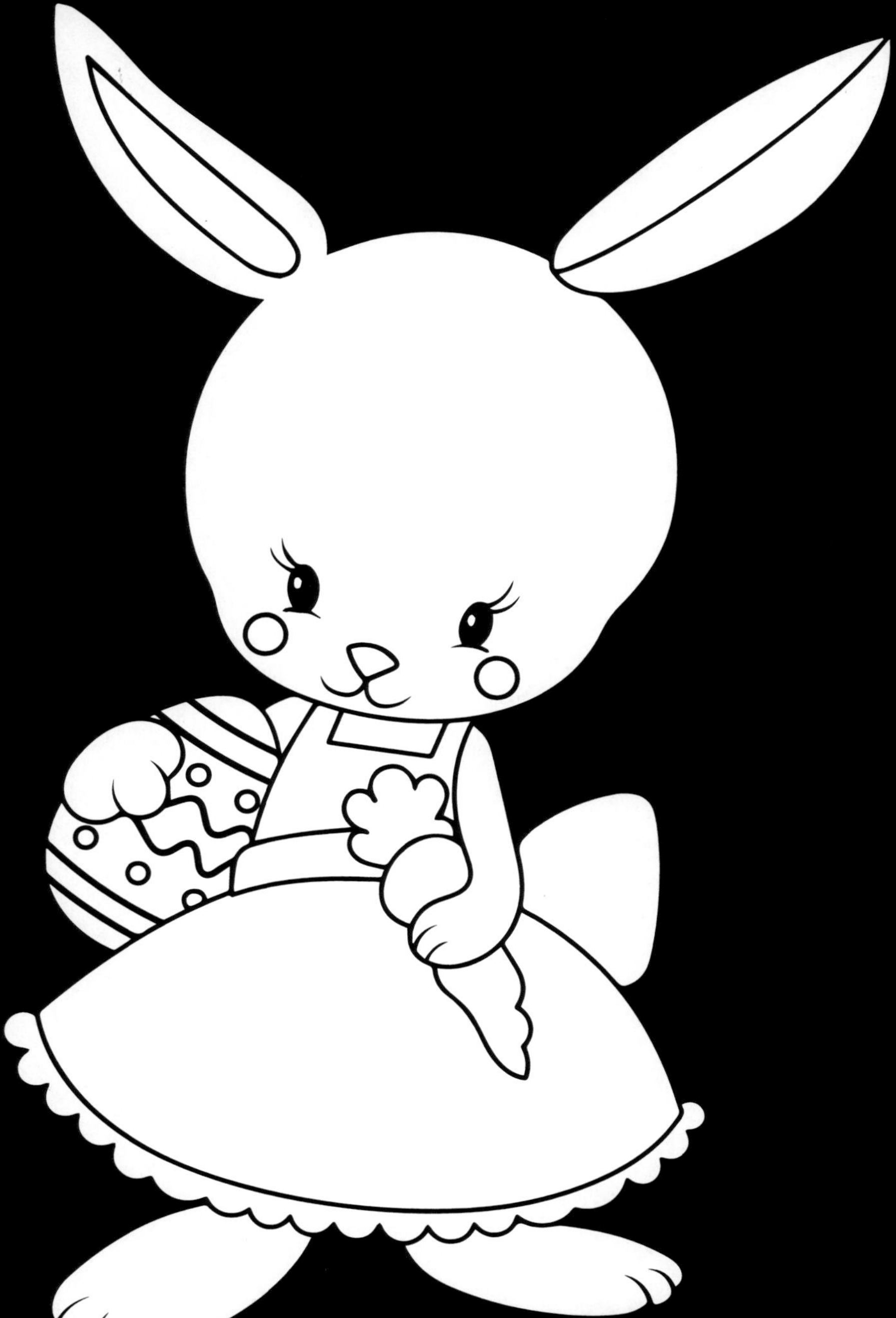

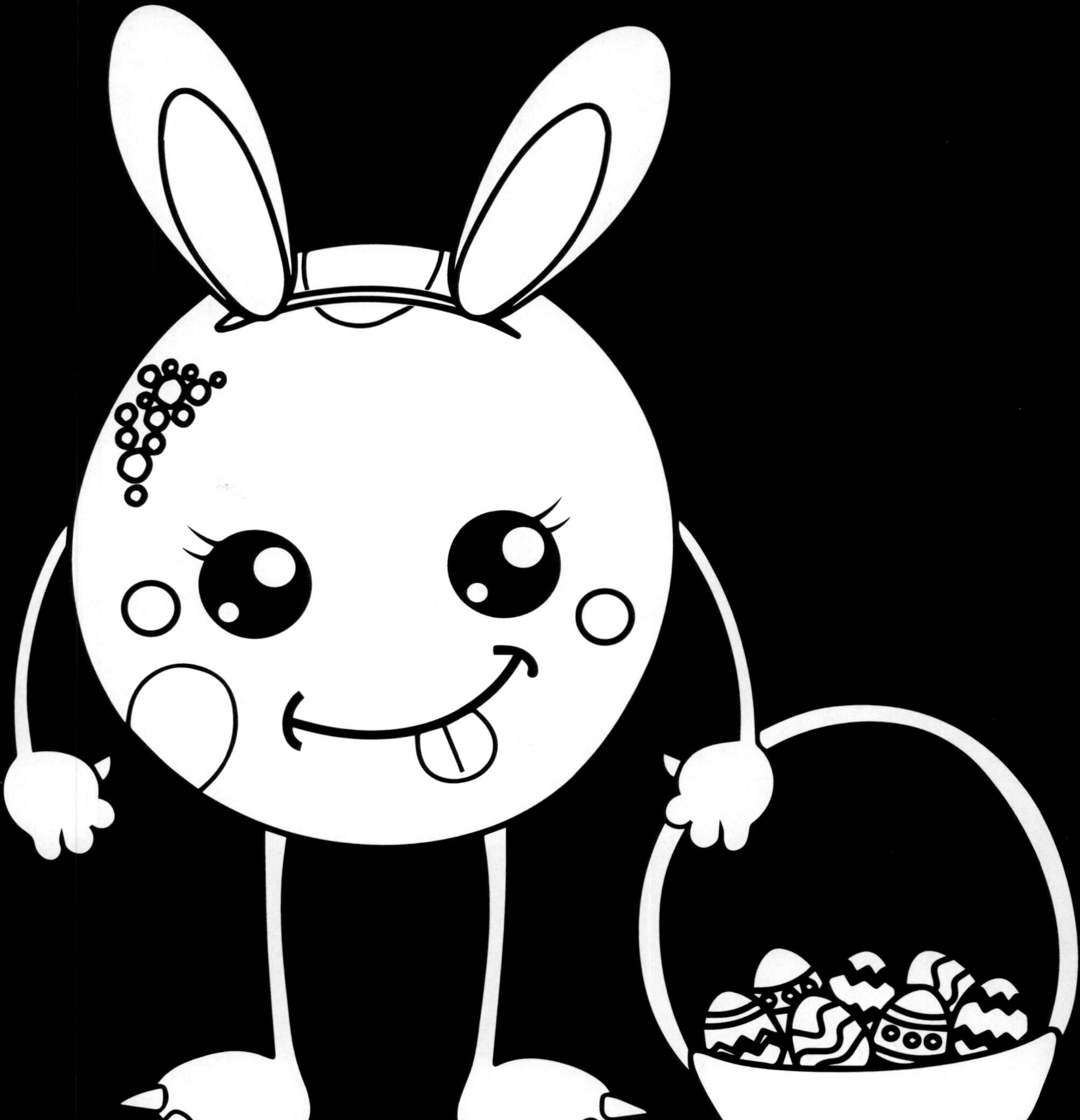

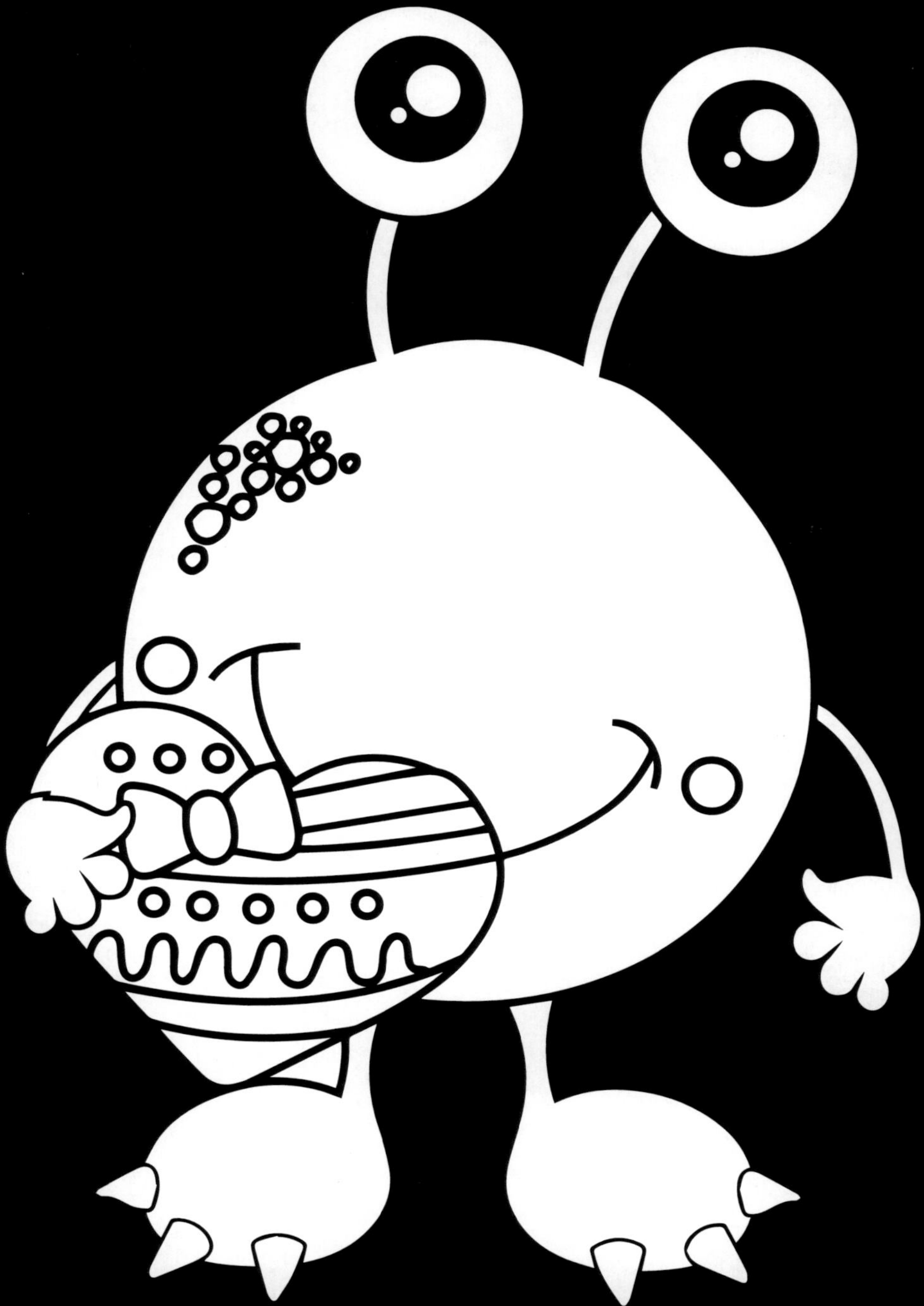

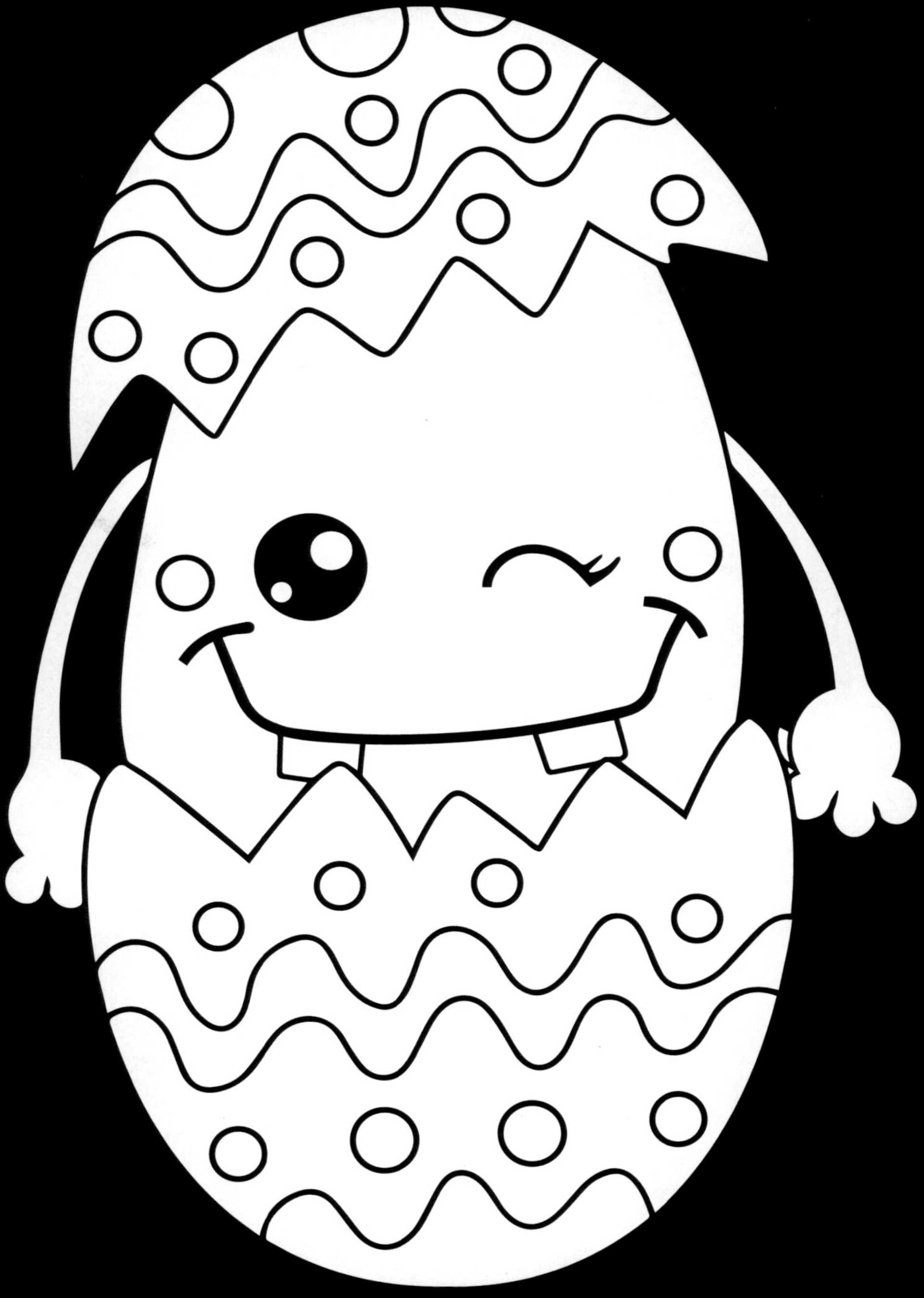

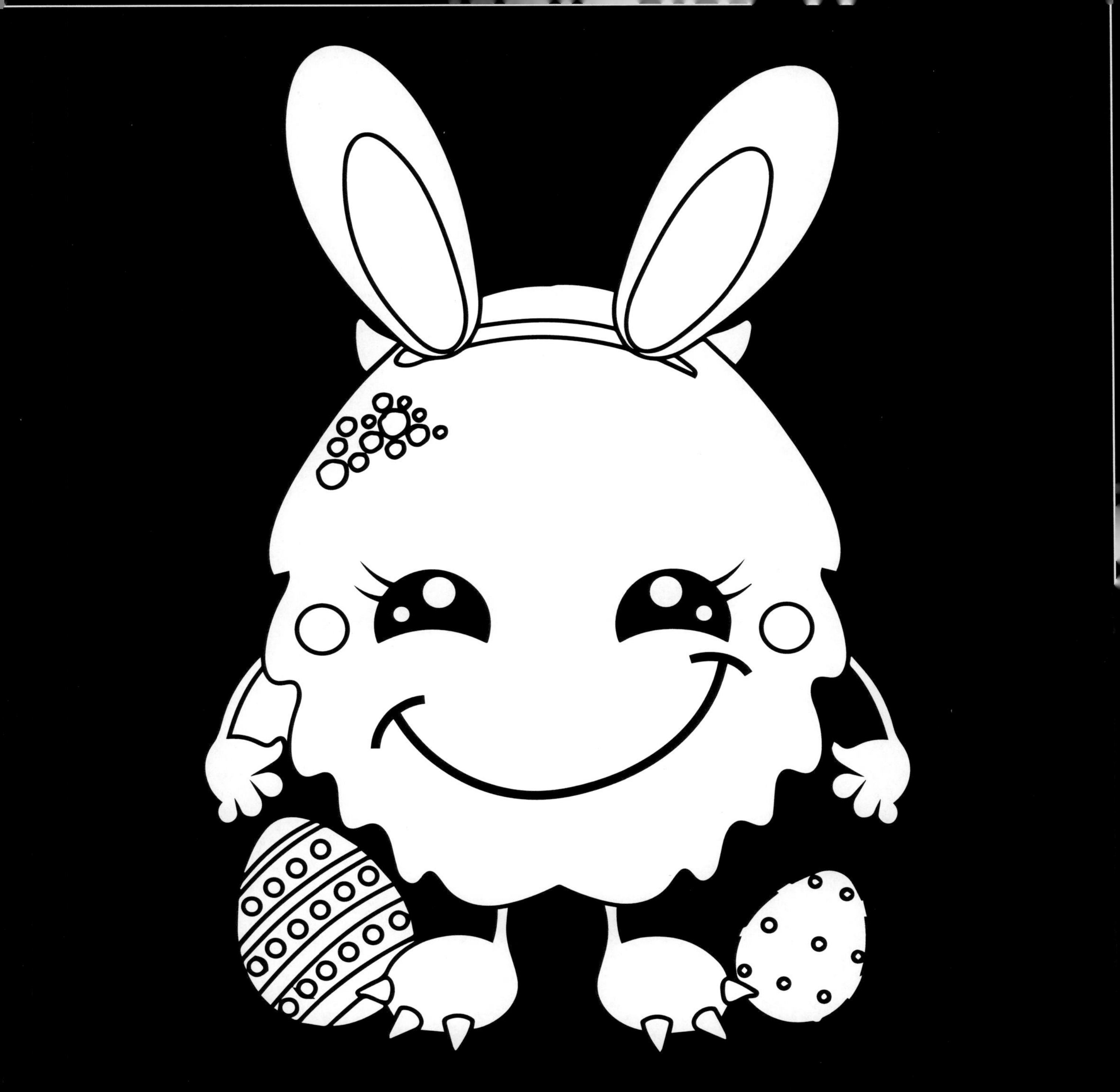

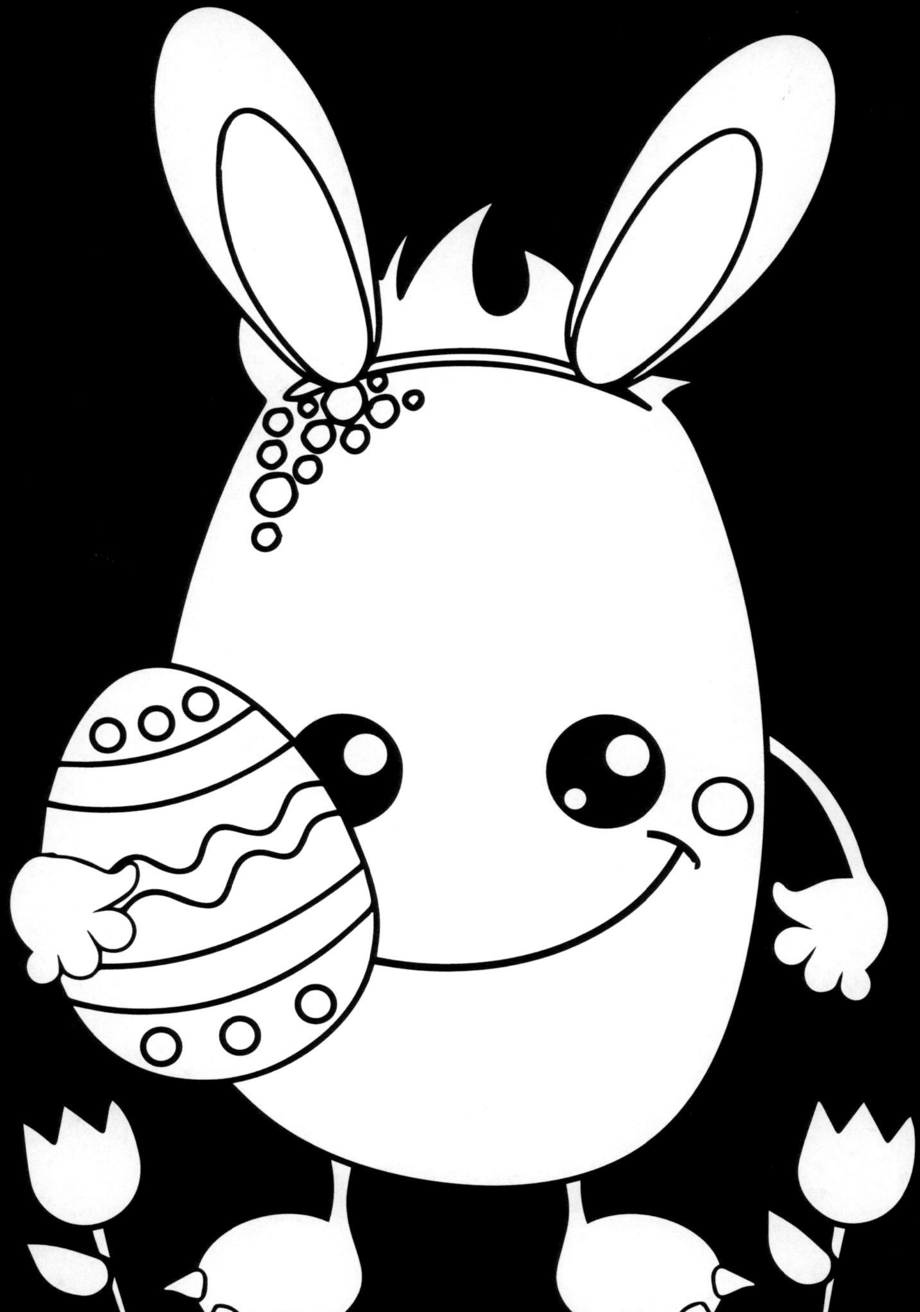

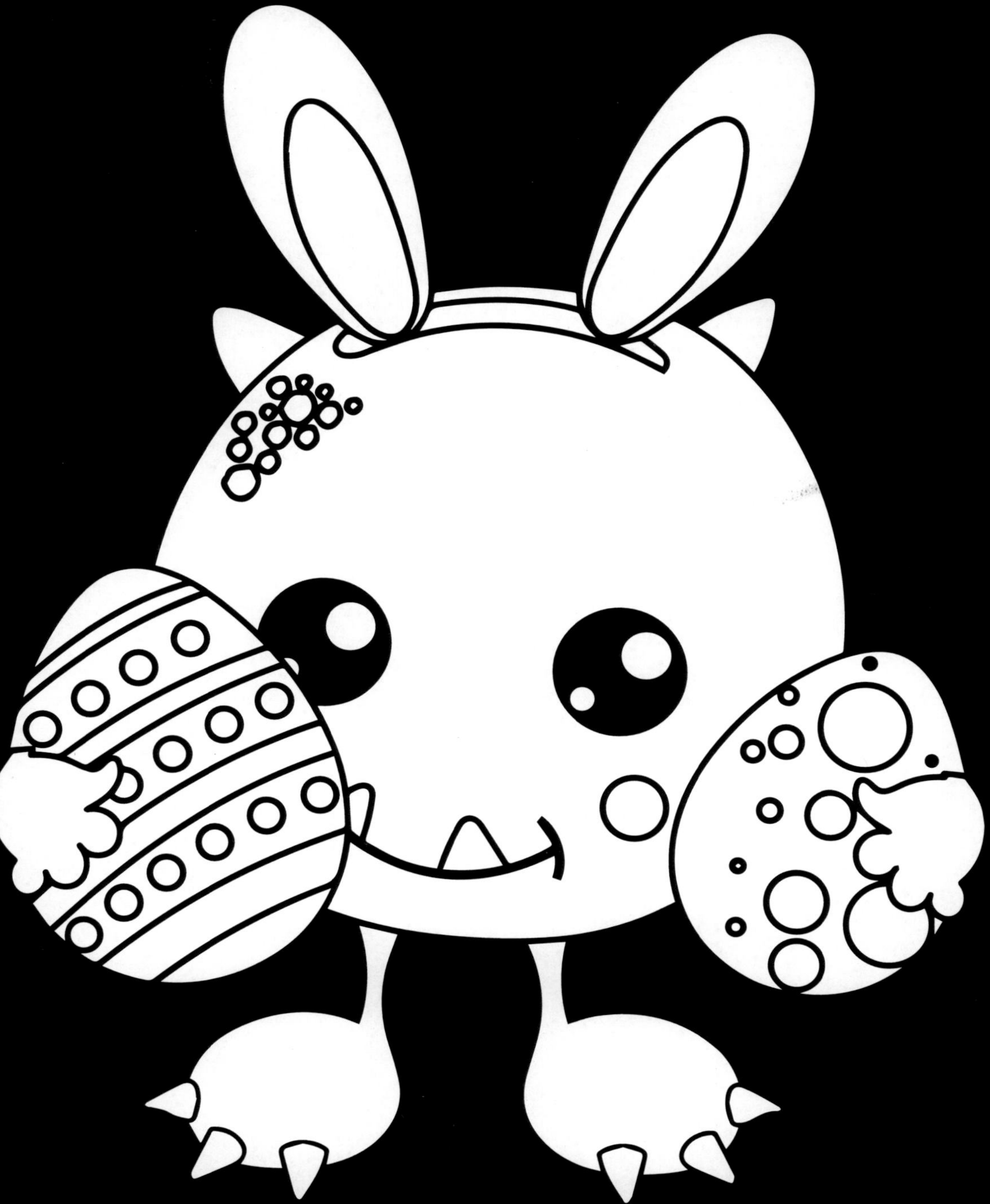

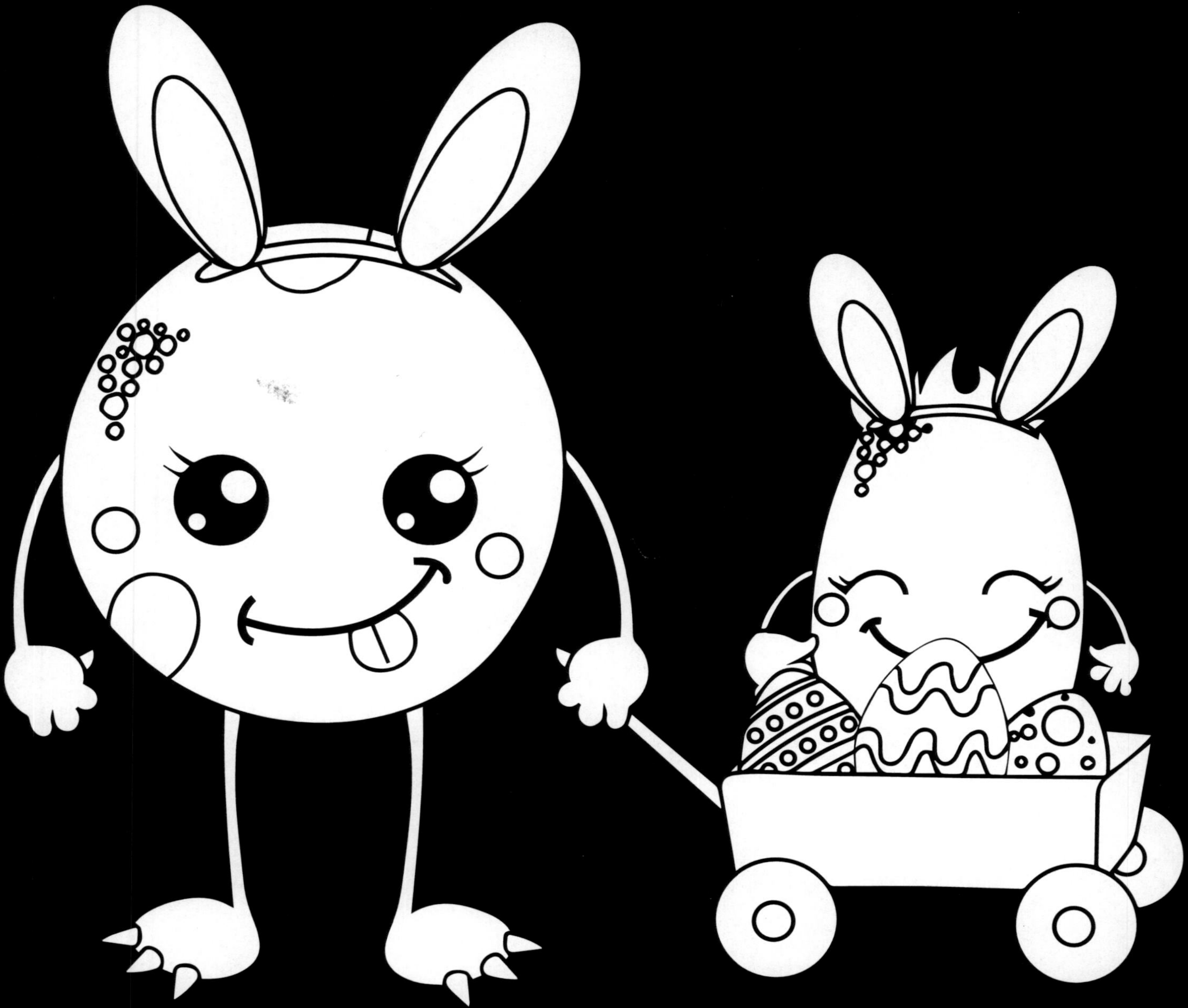

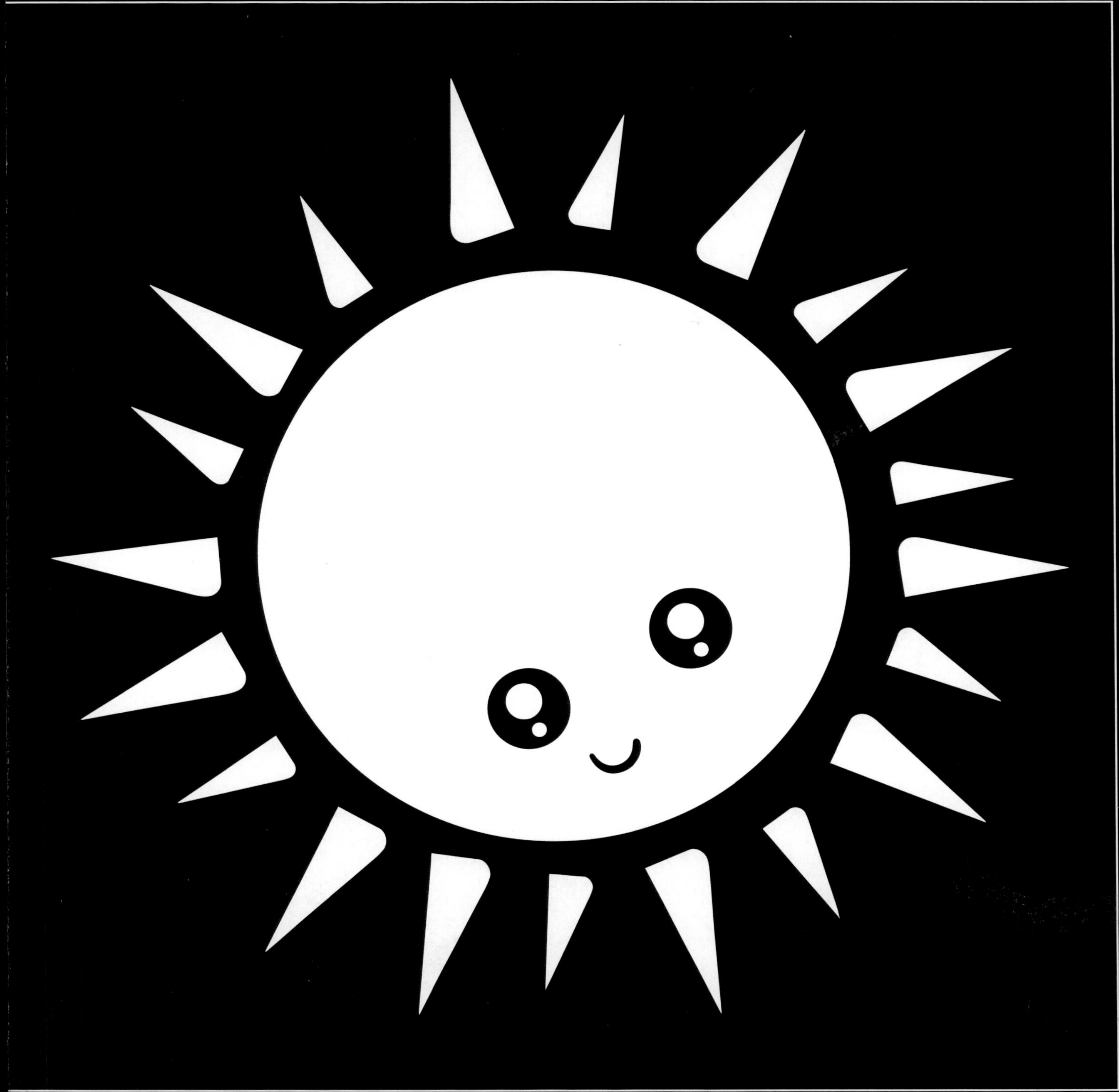

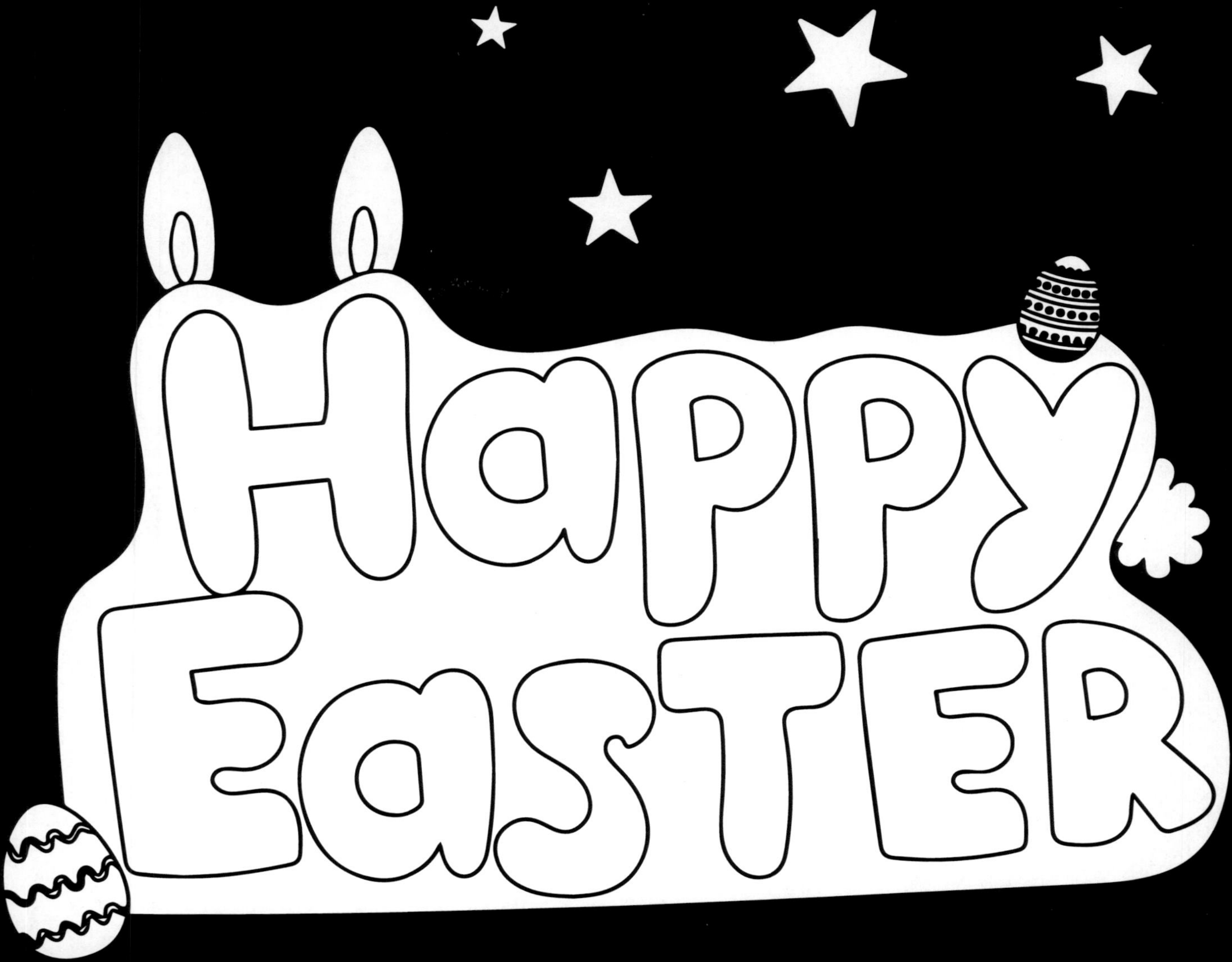
Happy Easter

Made in United States
North Haven, CT
15 April 2022

18305046R00017